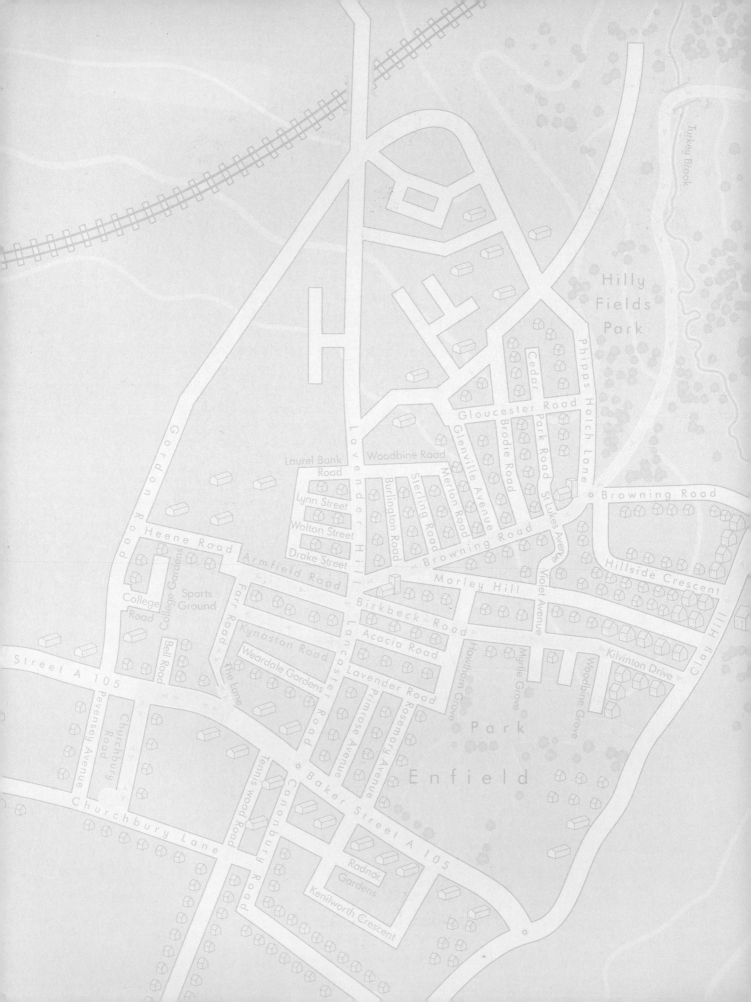

Bike Ride

Deborah Chancellor
Photography by Chris Fairclough

W
FRANKLIN WATTS
LONDON • SYDNEY

This edition 2005

Franklin Watts
96 Leonard Street
London
EC2A 4XD

Franklin Watts Australia
45–51 Huntley Street
Alexandria
NSW 2015

Copyright © Franklin Watts 2002

ISBN: 0 7496 6110 0
Dewey Decimal Classification 912
A CIP record for this book is available from the British Library

Printed in Malaysia

Series editor: Sarah Peutrill
Series design: Peter Scoulding
Design: Hardlines
Photographs: Chris Fairclough
Consultant: Steve Watts

Maps reproduced from Ordnance Survey mapping with the permission
of the Controller of Her Majesty's Stationery Office, © Crown copyright

With grateful thanks to the Bysh family

Contents

Checking the Map

The Bysh family are about to go on a bike ride. They have planned a **circular route**, starting and finishing at their home.

The family live in Enfield, in North London.

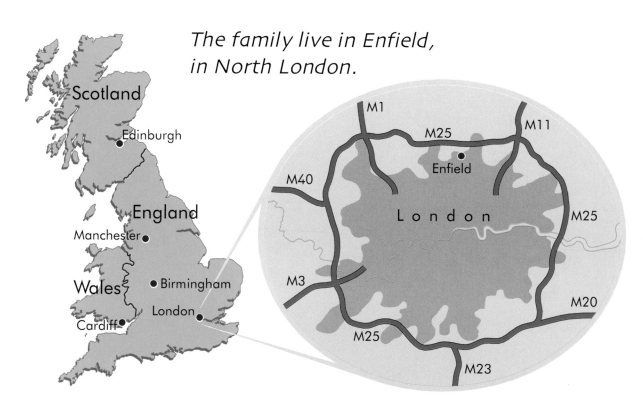

London is England's capital city.

On the route, they will cycle along busy roads and quiet country lanes. They will see lots of different things along the way.

It is important to check your bike is safe before you set off on a journey.

Dad tests the brakes on the children's bikes.

Mum and Dad check the map together.

Follow the maps in each section of this book to see where the Bysh family go on their bike ride.

Setting Off

Time so far: 1 minute. Distance: 200 metre

Mum, Dad, Sam and Sarah get on their bikes. They set off, cycling down Churchbury Road. There are houses on both sides of the road, and lots of parked cars.

CHURCHBURY ROAD EN 1

The street is quiet, but the family must still remember to cycle safely. They ride along in single file.

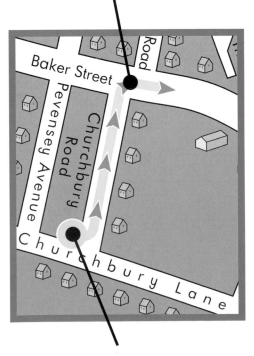

At the end of Churchbury Road they stop to turn right. They must take special care, because they are about to join a busy **high street** called Baker Street. There is more traffic on this road.

Mum signals to show she is going to turn right.

They turn into Baker Street here.

They start their journey here.

Maps have small symbols to illustrate important and interesting features. These symbols are usually explained next to the map in a **key**. Here are some symbols you will see on the bike route maps in this book.

 Direction of travel   Lake

Houses   Bridleway

Trees   Church

 Stream   Bridge

 Golf course   Roundabout

9

On the Way

Time so far: 4 minutes. Distance: 720 metre

The family cycle a short distance along Baker Street. Then they turn left into an **alleyway**. They walk with their bikes because this is a **footpath**.

The alleyway leads to a **side street** called Farr Road.

*This is a useful **short cut** for **pedestrians**.*

The alleyway is here.

They turn off Baker Street here.

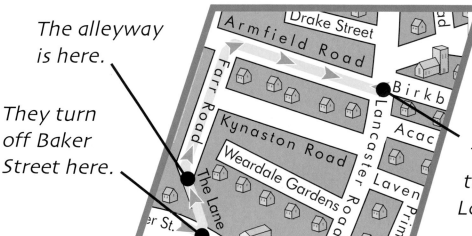

This is where the family cross Lancaster Road.

The family cycle along Farr Road and Armfield Road. These side streets are much quieter than the high street. Mum chose this route so they would not have to travel too far along the busy main road.

Soon they come to Lancaster Road, where there is a **shopping parade**. There is heavy traffic, so the family cross the road safely at a **pedestrian crossing**.

Can you see this church on the map?

Up a Hill

The family cycle up a hill. They have to change gear on their bikes.

BIRKBECK ROAD

Here is the street sign for the hilly road. Where is this road on the map?

12

The family see a park to their right as they cycle up the hill.

MYRTLE GROVE

The family turn right into Birkbeck Road.

About halfway up the hill, the family pass a park. The park gate is at the end of a **cul-de-sac** called Myrtle Grove. The children would like to stop and play in the park, but Mum and Dad just want to keep going!

Birkbeck Road

Acacia Road

Lane

Lavender Road

Primros

Rosema

Hawthorn Grove

Myrtle Grove

Woodbine

Park

field

The park gate is here!

Over a Stream

This is where the road goes over a stream.

The family turn left into a road called Clay Hill. They pass Bramley House Court on their right.

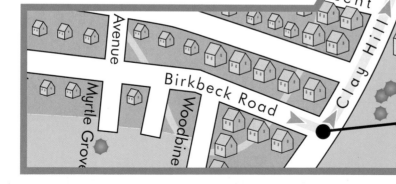

They turn left here.

BRAMLEY HOUSE COURT

This house is marked on the map because it is an interesting Victorian building.

At the bottom of Clay Hill is a bridge. The family stop here to look at the stream running under the road. This stream is called Turkey Brook.

This road is Clay Hill.

This area, as well as the road, is called Clay Hill.

The map on the right is taken from an **Ordnance Survey map**. It shows part of the family's route, just like the map on the opposite page. Can you see a thin blue line? This is Turkey Brook. Find the place where the road crosses over it.

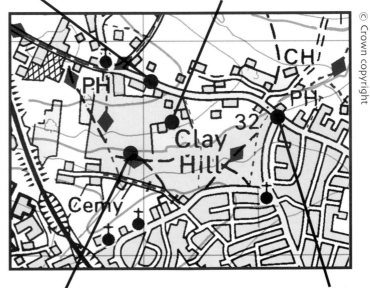

© Crown copyright

Follow this blue line and find where Clay Hill road crosses the stream.

They turn left into Clay Hill here.

Past a Golf Course

Time so far: 35 minutes. Distance: 3.05 kilometre

It's time to leave the busy roads behind. The family turn right into Beggars Hollow. This is a **no-through road**, which leads to Whitewebbs Golf Course.

They go over a bridge over a stream here.

The road ends here.

Whitewebbs Golf Course

Whitewebbs House and pub

Park Café

Beggars Hollow

Clay Hill

They cycle onto a **public right of way** through the golf course. There is no traffic here, so the family cycle side by side.

Suddenly, it feels like they are out in the country. The view is pretty and it is very quiet. The family cycle up another hill towards some woodland.

This section of the Ordnance Survey map shows Whitewebbs Park and Golf Course. Can you see the small symbol that means there is a golf course here?

The green area on the map tells you where the woodland is.

The tree symbols give extra information. They are curvy in shape, which means that the trees in this wood lose their leaves in winter.

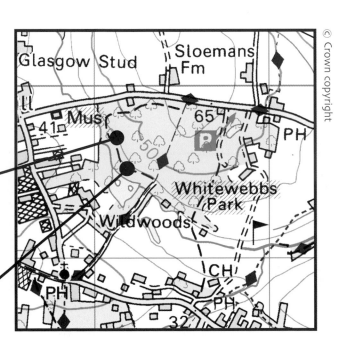

© Crown copyright

On the Bridleway

Time so far: 47 minutes. Distance: 3.98 kilometre[s]

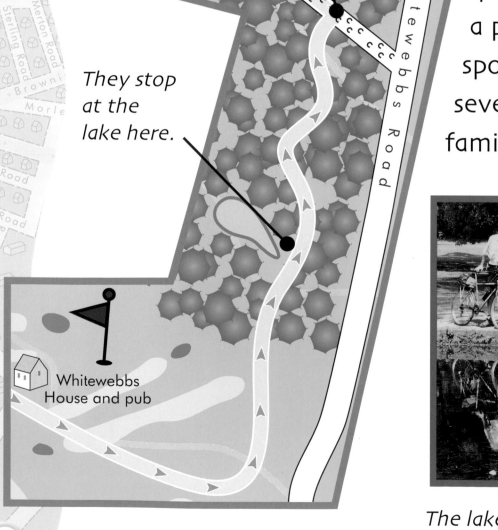

The family join the bridleway here.

They stop at the lake here.

Whitewebbs Road

Whitewebbs House and pub

As the family cycle through the wood, they pass by a lake. It is a popular picnic spot and there are several benches. The family pause for a rest.

The lake is surrounded by trees

The family come to a **bridleway** sign, and they turn left to cycle along the bridleway.

Soon, they meet some horses coming in the opposite direction. They stop to talk with the riders, then continue through the wood.

Back on the Road

Time so far: 53 minutes. Distance: 4.74 kilometre

The bridleway ends at the edge of the wood. The family cycle out onto a narrow road called Flash Lane.

The family are glad to reach the smooth road after the bumpy bridleway.

The family arrive at a **junction** where Flash Lane meets three other roads. Opposite them they can see a pub. Can you spot it on the map?

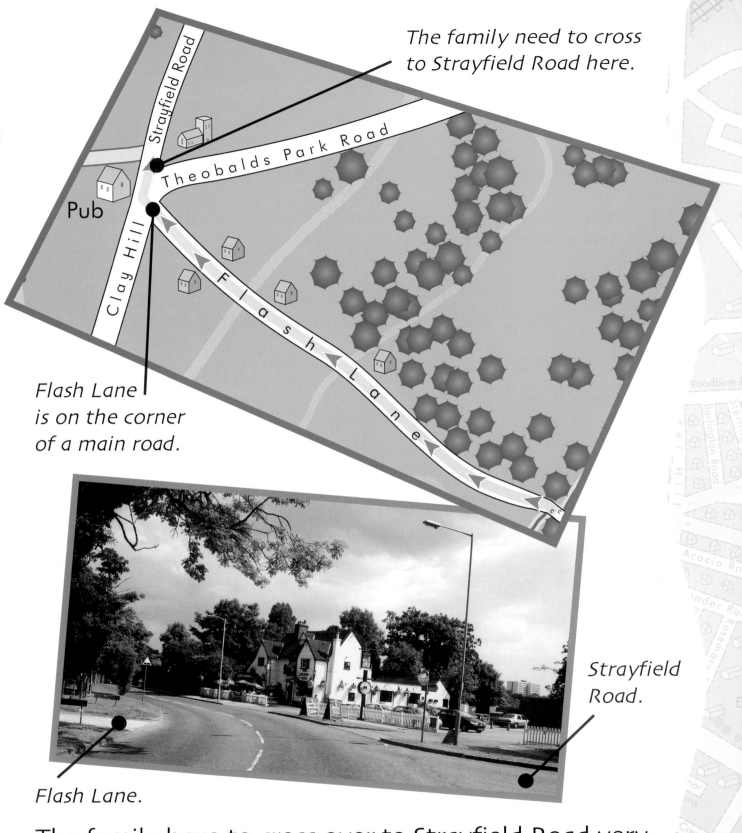

The family need to cross to Strayfield Road here.

Strayfield Road

Theobalds Park Road

Clay Hill

Pub

Flash Lane

Flash Lane is on the corner of a main road.

Flash Lane.

Strayfield Road.

The family have to cross over to Strayfield Road very carefully, because this is a dangerous **blind corner**. There is more traffic here than on Flash Lane.

Hilly Fields

Time so far: 1 hour. Distance: 5.91 kilometres

The family cycle through a park called Hilly Fields. They are off the roads once more. The park is very hilly, as its name suggests.

They go through some gates to get into the park. They cycle downhill first.

They cycle uphill to reach the corner of Phipps Hatch Lane.

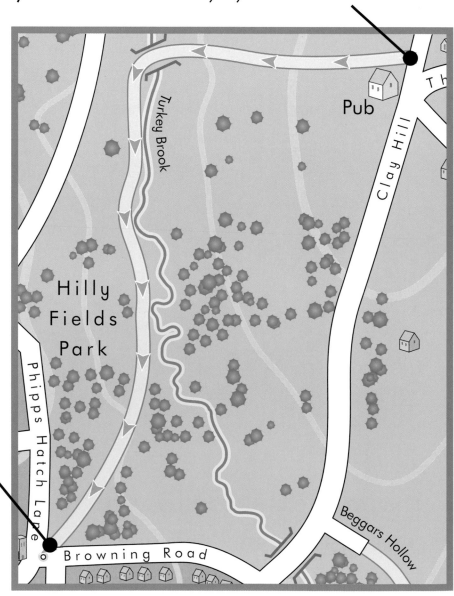

On this Ordnance Survey map, Hilly Fields is part of Clay Hill which is the area shown in grey.

Look at the pink lines. They are **contour lines**. Contour lines join together places that are the same height above sea level. When contour lines are close together like this, it means there is a steep hill.

What do you think it means if the contour lines are far apart?

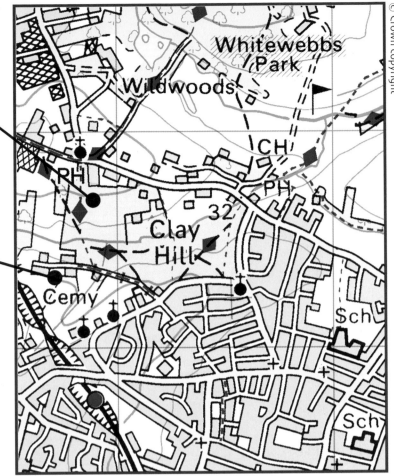

The hills are steepest on the way out of the park.

Returning Home

After leaving the park, the family join Phipps Hatch Lane at a **mini roundabout**.

Mum indicates they are turning right down Browning Road. This will take them back to the shopping parade on Lancaster Road.

© Crown copyright

Look at the church symbol on the Ordnance Survey map. This stands for the church you can see in the photo. The family use this **landmark** to help them find their position on the map.

24

It is downhill all the way from here.
Now the family go back almost the same way they came, cycling in the opposite direction.

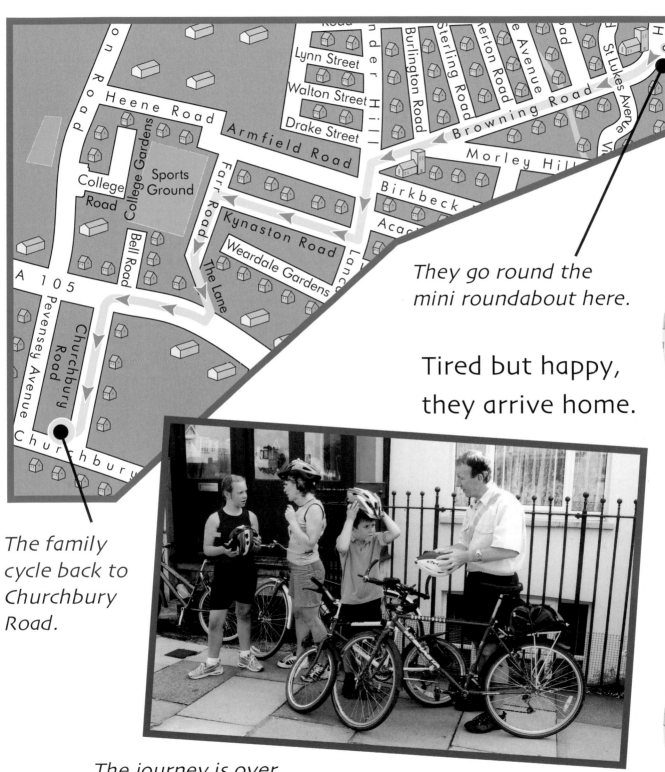

They go round the mini roundabout here.

Tired but happy,
they arrive home.

The family cycle back to Churchbury Road.

The journey is over.

Follow the Map

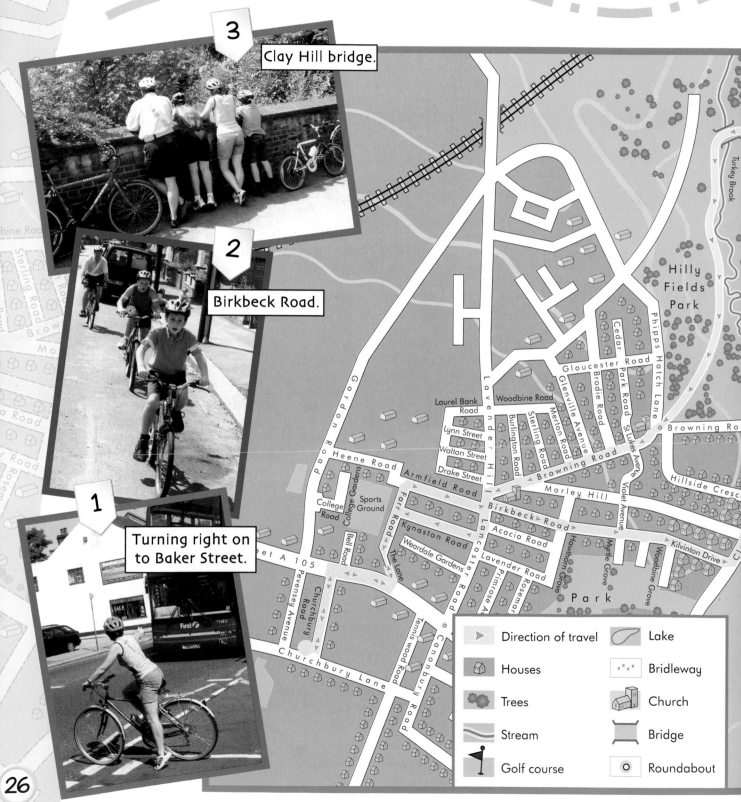

3 Clay Hill bridge.

2 Birkbeck Road.

1 Turning right on to Baker Street.

▷ Direction of travel		⬯ Lake	
🏠 Houses		ᶜᶜᶜ Bridleway	
🌳 Trees		⛪ Church	
〰 Stream		⊟ Bridge	
⚑ Golf course		⊙ Roundabout	

This is the circular route that the Bysh family took. You can follow their whole journey on the map. Look at all the different roads, junctions, paths and places they passed on their way. Now find where each photo was taken on the map.

Theobalds Park Road
Strayfield
Clay Hill
Pub
Flash Lane
Beggars Hollow
Whitewebbs Park
Park Café
Whitewebbs Golf Course
Whitewebbs House and pub
Whitewebbs Road
Cuffl

4 Through the golf course.

5 On the bridleway.

6 Phipps Hatch Lane roundabout.

Activities

Work it Out

1. Look at page 8. What are the family wearing and doing to make sure they are safe on their bikes?

2. Look at pages 16-17. How has the landscape changed since the start of the family's bike ride?

3. Look at page 22. How can you tell from the map that this part of the route is hilly?

4. Look at the different types of roads, paths and tracks the family cycle along on their route. Which do you think is best for a cyclist, and why?

5. Look at the map on pages 26-27. Can you work out a different route to Whitewebbs Golf Course?

Plan a circular bike route

- Look at a map of your local area. Find where you live.
- Plan a route for a bike ride, starting and finishing at your home.
- Try to pass lots of different features of the local area.
- Draw a map showing your route.

Glossary

alleyway
A narrow passageway that links two roads.

blind corner
A sharp bend in a road, where it is dangerous or difficult for people to cross because you can't see round the bend.

bridleway
A path that can be used by horseriders, cyclists and walkers.

circular route
A journey that starts and finishes at the same place and most of the route is passed only once.

contour lines
Lines on a map which join together points at the same height above sea level. They show how steep the ground is. When contour lines are close together, the land is very hilly.

cul-de-sac
A dead-end road.

footpath
A path to walk on.

high street
A main road in a city, town or village.

junction
The point where different roads meet.

key
A map key explains what all the symbols on the map mean.

landmark
Something that is easy to recognise.

map symbol
A small picture that represents or stands for something.

mini roundabout
A road junction where traffic goes around a small circle in the road.

no-through road
A road that doesn't lead to any other road, i.e. same as a cul-de-sac.

Ordnance Survey map
A detailed map that gives lots of information about the features of an area.

pedestrian
Someone who is walking.

pedestrian crossing
Traffic lights where people can cross the road safely.

public right of way
A path, road or track that anyone can use.

shopping parade
A row of small shops.

short cut
A route that is shorter and quicker than another one to the same place.

side street
A minor road in a town, often in an area where people live.

Victorian
From the time when Queen Victoria reigned (1837 – 1901).

29

Index

About this Book

FOLLOW THE MAP is designed as a first introduction to map skills. The series is made up of familiar journeys that the young reader is encouraged to follow. In doing so the child will begin to develop an understanding of the relation between maps and the geographical environment they describe. Here are some suggestions to gain the maximum benefit from BIKE RIDE.

It is important to emphasise road safety, especially with children who may be learning to cycle on roads. Talk about how the family in the book do all they can to ensure their safety, such as wearing helmets and fluorescent straps, cycling in single file, crossing over roads carefully and planning a sensible route along quiet roads.

In this book, some basic geographical concepts are introduced, for example contour lines. To reinforce understanding of these concepts, it will help to discuss local examples if possible, looking at maps of the local area.

Throughout the book, different examples of road and path are featured. Pick out some examples and discuss how they differ in terms of traffic frequency and land use.

On page 9 map keys and some map symbols are explained. It may be helpful to look at a broader range of symbols in a map key (such as those on an Ordnance Survey map) and find examples of them on the map itself.

On page 25 the church in the photo is described as a landmark. Talk about landmarks in your area, and find them on a local map. Describe where particular places on the map are in relation to one chosen landmark.

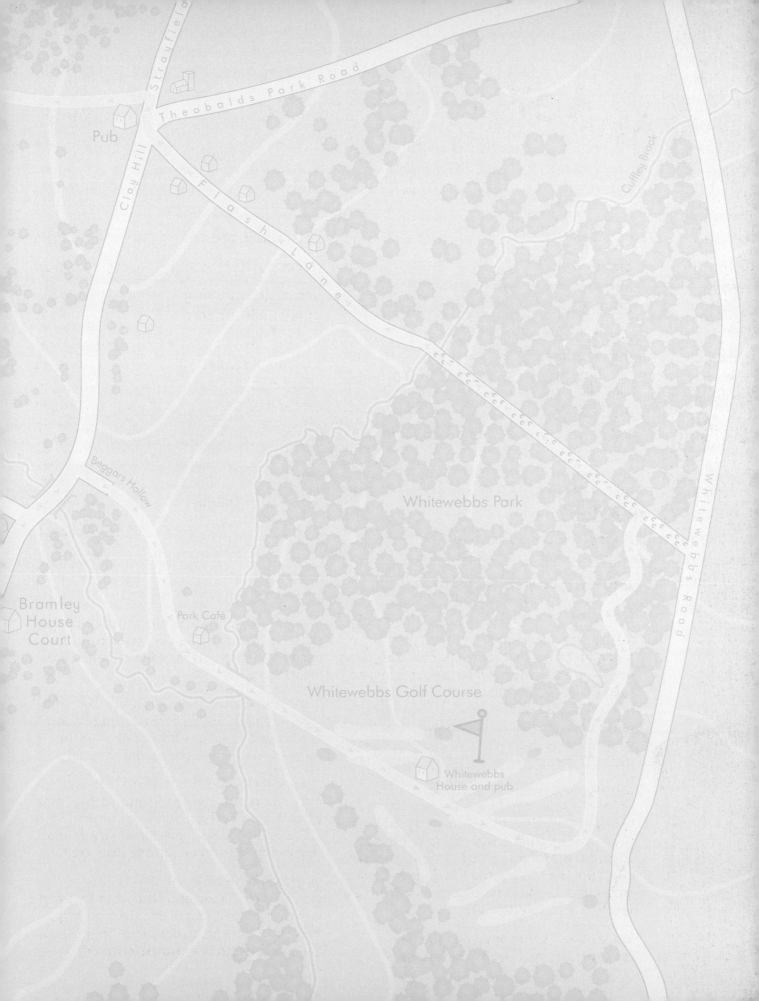